I want them to read like how they exist in my head.

I want to create a catalog full of flashes from encounters and observations of Nature.

I want to put the Big Picture on a stamp.

I don't know what the assistant should say. Perhaps that he has a portfolio full of ponderously written flashes from encounters and observations of Nature. Not essays, yet not poems either. Other than that, I'm not sure. Maybe when the puzzle takes shape, the picture will be more clear. Otherwise, thanks for the feedback and insight. I should go now, a few more flashes just appeared.

Love you, takecare, 2'

BULLETHEAD

A first pet is very important. No matter what it is, it will teach you responsibility and respect for all Life. Even if the scenario doesn't go so well. I remember my first pet. I essentially adopted him at our family's lake cabin. We had a neighborhood dog that wandered from house to house looking for food, but I had nothing of my own, and I thought I was ready. What I eventually found wasn't a soft, furry, cute thing that purred or barked. It was an ugly little bullhead fish. I loved that ugly little guy. I made him my pet because I caught him and didn't want to kill him. A couple days later I killed him.

> **He was small, ugly, & smelled bad; but he opened the door to my commitment to all animals.**

It was a neglectful accident, but where do you put a little bullhead fish. I chose a one gallon ice-cream bucket. My parents didn't want him in the house, so I put him on the back porch. Fresh air, clean water, good living. A nice thought, but I didn't figure in the fact that it was summer. Unfortunately, I practically boiled him like a lobster. Lessons are not always pretty things.

I regret only one thing. I didn't know enough and I didn't have him long enough to give him a name. So, this many years later, and many pets later, I've decided to call him Bullethead. He was small, ugly, and smelled bad; but he opened the door to my commitment to all animals. He also taught me that unless your pet is a tortoise or parrot, you're going to experience saying good-bye. Pets will always enhance our lives, but they will also leave our lives. So, for now, treats to all the good girls and boys.

A DATE WITH AUTUMN ────────────

Last night I went on a date with Autumn. She arrived last evening wearing the radiance of a translucent Full Moon. I was attired more commonly but it was darker where I stood. We've seen each other around, nodded acknowledgement, even spoken before; but last night we were somehow intimately familiar. I spoke first with obvious unease and inexperience, but she held her gaze and denied herself the comfort of hiding behind a tree or cloud. I actually did most of the talking and with her earnest listening and genuine responses a tolerable balance between unlikely lives was obtained. Shortly, she led the way as we timelessly waltzed toward her Western destination. Our full dialogue of simple visuals, sublime nuances, and subtle thoughts would be grossly underestimated at a thousand to one.

> **I quietly bowed and kissed her forehead good night.**

During those moments of silence between thoughts I would savor the sounds of the Night. I noticed the loud, piercing howl of the coyote chorus was absent; and replaced by the softer serenade of the cricket. When we would pass through an opening of the canopy her aura would flash like a lightning strike and illuminate the otherwise dim woods. I would try to take advantage by regaining a bearing on our path, but instead I would usually just notice the Fall leaves dropping amongst us. I was so smitten during our stroll I kept thinking the leaves were large rose pedals tossed before us by my fibrous friends. As I watched her more closely with every rosy step I suspiciously sensed her friends behaving coyly as well. Looking at the nearby constellations

it seemed like the tiny speck of the stars would glide a light—year closer for a better listen.   These moments of enchantment always make an impossible reality undeniable. Thus, last night our illicit affair became such reality when we made the trees chivalrous and the heavens jealous. As our stroll neared its unfortunate end I dared the obvious. With my last opportunity and as she floated into full sight, I quietly bowed and kissed her forehead good night. She paused for acceptance then gracefully continued on. I was momentarily paralyzed by her cosmic everything. I stood amazed at discovering that a brief moment of a beautiful something trumps any lasting void of anything. I simply turned and walked back through the dim woods just a man with a knowing grin under the evening moonlight.

There's a difference between an insect and a bug. An insect is simply a small invertebrate with a segmented body. A bug is simply an annoying little monster that won't stop buzzing your head and biting your legs. I like most insects . . . but I hate all bugs.

The hate-hate relationship between man and bug thrives nowhere more than when you're camping. And by camping I mean living in the woods weeks at a time with a dog you consider your best friend. Eating cattails, berries, and dandelions really makes you feel connected and grounded. Slapping your head all day just makes you feel victimized and crazy. I eventually had a solution to avoid the buzzing and biting.

The method was effective, just not really a public friendly solution. The basic problem was that the gnats and mosquitoes work together like a pro-wrestling tag team. The gnats will attack the head, and mosquitoes will go for the ankles and legs. Unless you're an octopus, you can't swat all the relentless little monsters. So, you're left to devise a method to fool them.

My particular method wasn't unique by any means. I'm pretty sure the idea came to me because my ancestors had used it for centuries. The process involved taking off your stinky t-shirt and tying it to an eight foot branch. Then you smear mud all over your face and torso and strap the branch to your back. The gnats will go for the stinky high point of the branch, and the mud helps save your skin from the mosquitoes. The unfriendly to the public part begins with the sight of a shirtless guy smeared with mud and walking with an eight foot branch on his back.

Actually, its not really public unfriendly until you accidentally walk upon a young family fishing at the local public access dock. When you walk up to a family of three and none of them move or blink for **I like most** over a minute—explanations are in order. **insects** In their eyes you could see confusion, fear, **...but I hate** and a sense of being on the cover of **all bugs.** National Geographic. I started to explain, but apparently they had to be somewhere because they all just ran to their car and left. Oh well, they left with a good story and I had many less buzzings and bitings to deal with. Solutions sometimes surpass the problem, but not when it involves bugs.

Three days before Christmas my frustration peaked. I had in mind to adorn my remaining gifts with feathers, but our local flying feather supplier was off hunting for his family in a squirrelier grove of trees. Without authentically gotten feathers my gifts couldn't bear the wanted synergy. If I wished my final few gifts to be truly authentic, then I was out of options. Except, perhaps, one impossible option. I could ask a certain love of my life, whose existence I doubt less than my own breathing, that if she was truly my everlasting partner then she would deliver up some needed feathers. As soon as I even thought it I dismissed the wish with shame. She has proven her existence so thoroughly, and has already provided me so much, that challenging her reality was overtly selfish and truly the only impossible option. Besides, my celestial partner can offer up such things as inspiration and contentment; but hardly could she provide the same material gifts as our active bird of prey. Thus, on the afternoon of the holiday eve, to the store we went, then to our gathering of friends and family.

As usual, we stayed overnight at the parental Pershing compound. The following daybreak, I woke with first light to walk with my fourpawed companions. We stepped outside and walked directly into the spectrum of a wonderful morning—bright, crisp, and invigorating. We inhaled the morning and hiked out onto the frozen lake where we could fetch snowballs, play tag, tug-on-glove, and search for mythic reindeer tracks. Then suddenly time stopped and the surrounding landscape blurred. We had somehow stumbled over a crease in the Cosmic fabric. Sight became smell, sound became touch. The mesmerizing moment passed and my regained focus noticed the dogs had all ran to a single object in the snow. I ran over to investigate and found a single wing. One fully intact wing of pristine feathers wrapped in a drift of untouched snow. No predator tracks, no signs whatsoever; nothing but an impossible present lying in the middle of a frozen lake. Awestruck numbness. With

No predator tracks, no signs whatsoever; nothing but an impossible present lying in the middle of a frozen lake.

tears of disbelief crawling down my face, I stared skyward and asked in our private silent language, "why?, no need." Quickly and quietly on a warm breeze her answer was delivered, "you couldn't, I could." With humble acceptance, I got my authentic Christmas Feathers.

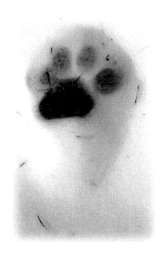

Mikko knew our situation might be trouble. We were hiking with two other dogs who were basically defenseless. One was a foster puppy named Fritzgerald, and the other was Mikko's little beagle house sister Roxanne. Our situation was dire because we were hiking at dusk on the upper cornfield. We went up there because it's a great arena to view the Full Moon. The problem, or mistake, was we weren't the only ones to think that. The coyotes thought the same thing, and they get pretty upset when strangers crash their moon party.

As soon as we heard them howl we entered our situation. Coyotes have been known to dig under and climb over twenty foot fences to get at a family dog. They don't enjoy humans that much, but if a tall-walker is out in the open with several dogs, there's not much hesitation.

Mikko was the one to think of a solution. He has wolf blood flowing in his veins, and he frequently would laugh at the coyotes. He called them little sissy pack hunters. The instant we heard the howling, Mikko turned and looked me right in the eyes. He was speaking and I understood him. He was telling me to get his sister and the puppy back home. He was going to distract the little sissy pack hunters. Mikko turned back around and sprinted directly into the middle of the coyotes. I ran the other two back home with confidence that my alpha male knew what he was doing.

The instant we heard the howling, Mikko turned and looked me right in the eyes.

Being the father of this courageous dog means I would worry for his safety half the night. I knew Mikko was good, and tough, but there was a lot of howlers. Could he really run right into the middle of them and make it home? About 10:30 he answered that question. Mikko not only strolled up to the back porch, but he did it with a huge grin. I guess I should have been worrying for the coyotes.

Life with Mikko . . . never far from a laugh or a tear.

I didn't mean to scare him, but the color left his face anyway. He seemed like a normal guy on a normal day. Wake up, eat breakfast, shower, and go to work. Simple, routine, and uneventful. Until of course your job as a courier sends you to a wooded oasis in a small town. Then simple and routine becomes very eventful.

The dogs and I lived on fifteen wooded acres surrounded by soy and corn fields. That's why I called it our little oasis. At the time of the situation I worked with horses and was a dog border. But my hobbies leaned toward the artistic. I carved custom walking sticks, dabbled in stained glass, and wrote stories in a journal every night. During the day it was basically chores and maintenance. It was the maintenance that scared the guy.

I figured it might be better to just walk up to him. Wrong choice.

The most recent Spring flood had caused a lot of damage. Trees had fallen on almost every trail the dogs and I used. It was my job to clear them. So, with saw and axe in hand I went to work early that morning. Push and pull, chop and chop. About noon I heard a truck pull up the driveway. I had forgotten that I ordered some pottery clay four weeks previous. It finally arrived.

I walked back to the house to meet the courier. Unfortunately, the saw I had was stuck in the trunk of a tree, so I just carried the axe back with me. The natural process of chopping trees means you're going to get wood chips sprayed up on the face. It was also Spring which meant the bugs were awake and active. Life in the woods teaches you to not expose too much skin to the wood chips and bugs.

This was the portrait that scared the innocent courier. I was dressed in work jeans, a hooded sweatshirt, sweating from work, bleeding around the face, and carrying an axe on my shoulder. I didn't want to scare him so I didn't shout introductions from the bottom of the driveway. I figured it might be better to just walk up to him. Wrong choice. When he heard my footsteps he turned around. Remote area, hooded guy sweating with blood on his face and carrying an axe. The box of clay he was unloading dropped where he stood. As I tried to thank him the back tires on his truck were already churning up gravel from the driveway. I don't think he works for the courier anymore. In fact, I'm not sure he works for anybody anymore. I felt bad, but it was funny.

HICCUPS

I laughed so hard I gave myself the hiccups. Little puppy Dupp was always good for a chuckle and a milk-out-your-nose snort. Ever since I adopted Dupp at four months of age, he's been a clown. But the hiccups were the result of his first eye-witnessed display of slapstick.

Dupp was brought into our home where he had two older house-sisters waiting for him. He immediately became enamored with Roxanne and Shania. In fact, I had to put the two girls out in the kennel so Dupp and I could work on house training without Dupp trying to bite their tails. Somehow the separation inspired him. I promised him that once he did each of the basic commands five times successfully, and stayed off the furniture while unattended (and spied upon), then he could go outside with his sisters. His house training took about two days before becoming second nature. A helpful, yet dangerous combination is mischievous and smart. Outside training was next. Could he walk with us and not run off when unleashed?

He wasn't going to let his sisters out of his sight for one second. He went where they went, and they went where I went.

The next morning he proved once again training was a non-factor. He wasn't going to let his sisters out of his sight for one second. He went where they went, and they went where I went. I felt like a very undeserving genius. So I decided to take them to the upper meadow that was adjacent to a cornfield. It was a beautiful sunny Fall afternoon. To get there we had to cross a small creek. Shania simply leaped from bank to bank, Roxanne liked to tip-toe across, and Dupp was intrigued. Being part Lab, water was in his blood, so he was intrigued for about two seconds before he jumped in. He was in no hurry to get to the other side. He wanted his sisters to join him, but they both just looked at him with that's-my-dumb-little-brother expressions. Once I crossed, Dupp figured family was more fun than water. Up the hill and onto the meadow.

The cornfield was recently plowed, so it was all torn up and littered with large mud clumps. This set the stage for Dupps naive hyjinks. While up there Roxanne liked to sniff around and take an accurate mole census. Shania preferred to run around and challenge any willing rabbit to a paw race. Dupp vacillated between sniffing and running. I stood by as audience and supervisor. Then suddenly Shania scared up a pair of turkeys. Not graceful flyers, in fact they're more like very long hoppers. They took off from the weeds and flew just overhead in our direction. This was very exciting for Dupp. He ran towards them, and when they flew past him he turned to follow. He was so fascinated by these flying things that he couldn't take his eyes off them. This meant he also couldn't see where he was going. And where he was going was right into the

He stood for a moment to collect his bearings, then turned to me with a that-was-so-cool grin.

mud clump littered cornfield. He missed the first clump but the second one was like Titanic's iceberg. His front paws smacked the clump dead center. Picture what happens next in slow-motion. With his front paws stopped dead, the rest of him decided to keep going. The result was a complete front somersault. It was so complete he literally landed on all four. He stood for a moment to collect his bearings, then turned to me with a that-was-so-cool grin. I'm not sure what happened next, I was too busy trying to catch my breath. I'm just glad I wasn't drinking milk at the time.

GRANDFATHER ─────────────────

I call him GrandFather. He is old and grey. He can't sway and he has no bark so he's bald too. He's playfully domineering though: on any given day he'll creak loudly like he can't stand no more just as you walk beneath. He stands like a respected elder who many owe life and duty. One of his long ago seedlings has grown tall and holds his honored GrandFather up with strong outstretched

He showed us Nature's beauty and the will to survive.

limbs. On his downward slope no roots will take so he still claims a prime view of the creek. I imagine the days of his youth when he would reach and fight for sunlight. In his established years with trunk proudly expanded, he would help the eversearching predators hide in-wait for the everexpecting prey. For Cosmic balance he would in turn allow the nesting of friendly fowls. Not so long ago he would witness the journey of upright bipeds who walked with stealth and stoic intent. One of those bipeds would become a Chief and return after changing worlds to protect the special group of trees for as long as they stood. Then far too soon after GrandFather would witness the wasteful clearing of younger trees all around his family and he became bitter and sad. While living amongst his family I have tried my best to honor and respect GrandFather . . . he has not many storms left. I'll miss him and all my fibrous friends. Soon I wave good wind and steady light to Chief BrightFeather. I know they will stand proud to the end. My journey is onward to a new grove whom are watched over by EaglePine. May we be accepted and join in their secrets and wonders. No journey should be taken if a tree is not the destination.

Suddenly the little grey rock, sitting in the corner of the kennel, moved. What the? The dogs hadn't noticed, which was good; because four dogs and something small and moving makes not for a good scenario. I went closer to investigate and it turned its head. What I discovered was a tiny baby owl. The question was why and how did it get into the corner of the kennel? For the safety of our little grey rock with wings, I rushed the dogs into the house.

Not having a clue, I knew I should talk to somebody who could explain our peculiar situation. I called the Raptor Center. The helpful person I talked to, suggested it was perfectly normal. The peculiar situation indicated a Bard owl family. Apparently, the Bard owl nests in nooks of trees, not twig nests in trees. When baby comes along, space becomes limited, so they kick the baby out of the tree and take care of it on the ground. I soon found out that they not only care for it, but they protect it with violent prejudice.

The baby noticed, sat up and stared at me.

The raptor people said maybe to try and move the baby into an open area where the mother could find a better watching place. I then went and got a big shovel and entered the kennel. The baby noticed, sat up, and stared at me. I approached to see if I could get him on the shovel and move him at least outside the kennel. The little owl started clicking his beak and raising up his talons. A baby owl that could literally fit in the palm of an adult hand, also has a foot with talons the same size as an adult hand. Then the peculiar situation leaped from problem-solving right to major fear.

Think of a situation that you considered to be so frightening that your heartrate felt like a strobe-light in your chest. Then double it. When I was in the kennel with the baby I had only good intentions. Mother owl didn't see it that way. I was humped over trying again to scoop up the baby when mother owl swooped in. From about six feet above my head, an incredibly angry, vengeful scream rang throughout the woods. There was no "hoo hoo hoo"! Instead there was a loud "get the *%#% away from my baby"! I was startled, so turned my head around and looked up. All I saw was a six foot wing span with eight daggers for toes perched on the lowest and closest branch.

Her eyes were aimed right for my head if I did anything else. I put the shovel over my head and sprinted back into the house.

I watched through a window to see if our situation would have a happy ending. The mother stayed to guide her baby and it did eventually make it out the kennel door. We never saw the baby again. Good luck to any predator trying to get an easy meal . . . or to help move a little grey rock with wings.

He left on a Saturday, but he also showed up on a Saturday. Mikko had to show up because Simba had to leave. Simba was my cat. He was mistaken for a destructive stray by a frustrated apartment manager. Simba was also my bridge into the kingdom that exists somewhere between flora, fauna, and the up-right walkers. Our roles in Life are not to be chosen, they're just to be fulfilled. Mikko was on the other side of that bridge.

The bridge lead straight to the local Humane Society. Six aisles of kennels, about forty dogs total. A good place to start. Most of the dogs barking, some simply begging, and a few who had just given up. As I turned the corner of the second aisle there he was. He was calmly lying in the corner. He looked right into my eyes and gave a tiny head nod. I understood him. He was telling me to keep going and make sure I looked at all the others as well. I have never wasted so many footsteps my entire life. When I returned to Mikko he was calmly sitting at the door and waiting for the volunteer to unlock it. He knew . . . and I was learning. Absolute knowledge is not common, but when it shows up you don't blink and you don't think. You just click on the leash and wait to see who's leading who.

Absolute knowledge is not common, but when it shows up you don't blink and you don't think. You just click on the leash and wait to see who's leading who.

Once the leash was on, we went back to our van and our life together began in earnest. The first thing was to learn more about each other. We couldn't really exchange stories so we just spent a lot of time staring at each other. I don't know much, but I did learn not to get into a staring contest with an owl, or a dog that was really more than a dog. It was humbling to have to be the first to blink every time. Next came our names. He was called Mikko and I was called what my Mother and Father chose to call me. However, Mikko and I grew close to each other and eventually we discovered our true identities. We discovered them on the North Shore. Mikko was playful and whenever we found other dogs to play with I discovered I couldn't say his name out loud. When I would exchange dog stories with the other up-right walkers

Mikko would hear his name and stop playing to see what I wanted. The fact that I didn't want anything from him at the time simply annoyed him. Annoying your Cosmic mentor is never a good thing. Thus he acquired a nickname. Mikko became known as FourPaws. The other dog people figured it would only be fair if I acquired a nickname as well. I then became known as TwoFeet who walks with FourPaws. When the name fits, you wear it.

Next, FourPaws got kicked by a horse. I wanted to gain more of his trust so we went on a little trip. We loaded up the van and went to visit all the national parks and remote campgrounds we could find. And we found more than a few. But this one time, when we were just outside Wibaux, Montana, we drove past this big horse ranch. We

had been driving for quite some time and thought a quick stop to meet some new friends and stretch our legs would be nice. We pulled over next to a small coral with three horses in it. There was the daddy horse, mommy horse, and their little foal. We walked up to the fence and all three approached. I'm sure they thought we had treats. The mare and the foal seemed excited about having visitors. The daddy horse was a bit more suspicious. Mikko ran under the fence to sniff the strange, long-faced, fourhoofed walkers. The foal was willing to play. The mare decided to come over to me and see if carrots were involved in the visit. When Mikko made the foal rear-up, the daddy horse had had enough. He ran over to Mikko and kicked him like Gary Anderson in a SuperBowl. Mikko was alright, but he got the message: Rabbits and squirrels were a lot less hostile and had softer feet. Mikko and I continued our journey.

On and on we went. Many experiences, many lessons, and an evergrowing bond. We went to the hills of North Dakota, to the lakes of South Dakota, to the mountains of Montana. We went never as a man and his dog, but rather as simple partners and friends. Then came the time when we had to choose a home. We found it in south central Minnesota. We found a small wooded oasis amongst the corn and soy fields of the region. We found where we belonged.

They all had something to say and something to teach. My most important lesson was to speak less and listen more.

We belonged there because the trees said so. They spoke the language of the wind. To understand it required listening. However, they were speaking just to me. Mikko was already fluent in Nature's tongue. He was in my life to prepare me and make sure we got to the oasis. Mikko did his job well. Eventually our lives together became crowded. Soon we met Roon the Raccoon, Hemi the Hummingbird, the Bardolos the Owl family, Ellie the little green Frog, Kate the Coyote, Opus the Opossum, and Tate and Turk the Turkey twins. They all had something to say and something to teach. My most important lesson was to speak less and listen more. However, the more I listened the less Mikko had to teach.

It was a Saturday afternoon Mikko decided it was time to go. He had more students to meet and more tongues to teach the language of the Cosmos. It's humbling to have a dog that's really more than a dog teach you how to be a better human. Then again, animals are usually better teachers than humans anyway. Mikko was on the Run and I was left with the responsibility of passing on the message. So, speak less, listen more, and adopt a pet.

We never saw the first baby owl again. But, Ma and Pa owl were ever-present. They would swoop over the skylight at night, talk to each other to coordinate hunts, and seemed to follow us during hikes. We lived in a synchronous existence. The root of our agreement was based on survival. The dogs and I allowed them to hunt the sky and ground freely and we would leave them be. The owls responded by allowing our cats, Tan Tan and Pai Pai, to come and go without harm.

At first our existence was safe and mutual, but kind of vague. I admit though that it was pretty cool watching the owls scare off the hawks and crows, while the cats returned home walking directly up the middle of the driveway. A place where many moles and rabbits contributed to the ecosystem. The vagueness was erased when the second baby owl arrived.

I knew it wasn't an accident because on the trunk of a tree ten feet away perched protective MaMa Bard.

What happened with the first baby was simply a matter of misunderstanding. MaMa owl apparently wasn't going to let that happen again. I think it was a Tuesday morning. The dogs and I woke and grabbed some breakfast before our morning hike. I don't know exactly how she did it, but I guess she had watched us enough to know our routine. We descended from the loft and headed for the front door. I opened the door and scanned the yard, in case four energetic dogs bursting out the door might just catch somebody or something off guard. However, it was I who was caught off guard that morning.

Sitting on the front stoop sat the second grey rock with wings. I knew it wasn't an accident because on the trunk of a tree ten feet away perched protective MaMa Bard. Her stare told me that our little agreement was going to last just a bit longer. It's normal to bond with a family dog, cat, or horse; but having a clear understanding with a bird of prey is another entire level. I guess if you respect all Life weird things are bound to happen . . . just be prepared.

TOUGH BEAVER

Telling stories about surviving encounters with coyotes, bears, and wolves are impressive tales. But, being outsmarted by a beaver just leads to silent humiliation. My particular humility happened at a YMCA camp. I had been working there for a few years, and in almost every capacity. If a new program needed to be started, or pamphlets needed to be written, I was the guy. Unfortunately, I was also they guy who was responsible for solving problems. The beaver was a problem. He was chewing all the trees down on the lakes' shoreline. This caused erosion. This became my responsibility.

SEASON FLAVORS

Summer usually tastes like a hot sloppy joe...

Each season has its own flavor. Winter in Minnesota tends to be like cold pizza for a quick breakfast. Summer usually tastes like a hot sloppy joe; or on some days a warm fish casserole. Fall is a two day old turkey sandwich with fresh lettuce and

Even in undeveloped suburbs gunfire isn't permitted. Thus, I had to go to the trapping method. I went and purchased about five humane traps, so when I caught him he could be replaced many miles away. His daily trails were all pretty obvious, which I thought would make my job fairly easy. The beaver thought my job was fairly pathetic. I set the traps with some fruit and waited. When I returned the next day I found nothing trapped and no fruit. I reset the traps and moved a couple out to a small island. He wouldn't expect that. Well, he may not have expected it, but he did discover it. The following day, while I canoed out to check the island I was greeted with several sarcastic tail slaps on the water. He wasn't only smart, but very smug as well.

My problem was eventually solved by two unexpected allies. It turns out nesting geese are as protective as roosters and pitbulls. An angry goose is known to be able to break the neck of even a large hunting dog. The beaver was smart enough to know which battles are worth fighting. Dumb upright walker worth the battle, angry big birds not. He moved on. At least the geese didn't chew on the trees.

He wasn't only smart, but very smug as well.

tomato. Spring is generally muddy, but at least you don't have to shovel for an hour just to get out of the driveway. To me, Spring is a nice roll of sushi; preferably tuna, carrots, and jasmine rice. Fall is my favorite season, but no one can turn down a nice roll of sushi. Every season has its own flavor, but the trick is to learn to enjoy all the tastes that tingle the palate.

SNOWFLAKES AND STARS ————————

She composed songs in a language only she and the birds fully understood.

It was unclear whether the birds taught her, or she the birds.

The other day snow was falling gently to the ground. The other night stars were sparkling brightly in the clear sky. Today a sapling of an idea came to fruition when the two natural events combined to form one fantastical story:

There was this little girl who lived North of the Gateway to the North. She lived with Ma and Pa and the closest neighbors were the coyote, wolf, and moose. People came by once in awhile, but they usually were wearing bright orange, or a green uniform with a DNR patch on the breast. The family farmed organic mushrooms for co-ops, harvested earthworms for bait shops, and hunted for the state to feed the less fortunate. A simple life, a satisfying life. The little girl wasn't sad that no other kids were around to play with; nor did she hope to grow up faster so she could get away and move closer to others. She was happy to just be a kid with her own huge playground. Even in her youthfulness, she developed a vast imagination and an innate ability to contain a boundless sense of playfulness. Everyday she created twenty-five new games with whatever she found in the meadow or woods. She composed songs in a language only she and the birds fully understood. It was unclear whether the birds taught her, or she the birds.

One night she was sitting on the steps of the porch. The night was so clear, and so bright that it would have been easy to read

a book right then and there. She sat there looking up at the sky in fascination. Still too young for philosophical thoughts, she instead tried to count the stars, but kept losing track of which ones she had already counted. Then she started drawing dot-to-dot pictures. She even named some of her favorite stars, noting how different all of the stars were. The next morning she awoke to a gentle snowfall. She loved the snow just as much as the stars. She especially loved all the games to be played in the snow. Her favorite was running around her meadow with her mouth wide open trying to catch as many in her mouth as possible. With her head tilted up, trying to catch the snow, the vast gates of her imagination began to creak open. The snowflakes were the large soft type. She playfully held out her hand, and as the snowflakes landed on her mittens, she  noticed how different each snowflake was. Her mind traveled to the night before when she noticed the same thing about the stars. Some minds turn on a light bulb when an idea starts to take form, but at that moment her mind switched on flood lights.

She reckoned that if the snowflakes are so many yet so unique, and the stars are so many yet so unique, then they are different but also the same. Her only reference of this thought was her grandfather and her father. They too are unique, and different, but she saw them as the same hardworking person. Then she remembered a time last Fall when her grandfather became ill. While her grandfather rested, her father took over the farm. The grandfather was proud to be able to witness how well his son did with the farm, even though he did some things different. The little girl saw her grandfather leave as a proud father and grandpa (she never did like the word 'died').

So maybe when the old stars get tired or ill they hand over their job and come floating down to the ground.

Then she looked up to the sky, then down to the ground. Her maturing mind brought her to this: if the exchange of similar but different things happened in the Fall for people, then maybe the same happened for the stars in Winter. Maybe Winter wasn't just a cold, grey, lifeless season of snow games and dragon breath; perhaps it was the season of exchanging the old and new stars. Her mind was having fun now. She figured that the stars give us a beautiful night display, and she even heard that people in boats use them to find land. That sounds kind of like the work

needed to keep a farm healthy every day, and everybody with a job seems to hand it over to somebody else at sometime. So maybe when the old stars get tired or ill they hand over their job and come floating down to the ground. They must choose Winter because it's still cold and they can stick around a bit longer and rest awhile before 'leaving'. It made sense. The stars are unique, snowflakes are unique, and there must be about the same number of both. The little girl stood there and smiled because she knew she was right and nobody was around to dispute her.

She looked down at the ground again and a new love of snow and stars twinkled in her eyes. Suddenly a new thought came to her. She figured that the stars must have had a long trip from the sky, and they must miss their job a little bit. So, she looked around and picked up one of her favorite sticks and began running around her meadow poking holes all over. She wanted them to look like the stars she saw in the sky at night. When the meadow was full she started making dot-to-dot pictures everywhere. No warriors, or lions, or gods. They were retired now, so she chose flowers, smiles, butterflies, and candycanes. When her meadow was full she stood to the side and looked at her ground-sky, and she was satisfied. There were twice as many footprints as ground-stars, but she chose not to notice them. Since she was already smiling, she just turned and began walking back to the house for lunch. When she reached the porch she stopped and turned for a more distant look at her ground-sky. What she saw was a moonlit surface of a lake when the lake looked just the same as the sky; and if possible she smiled even wider because she knew she was right. She was proud that Winter and the snow and the stars made more sense to her today than they did yesterday; but

When her meadow was full she stood to the side and looked at her ground-sky, and she was satisfied.

her mind's vast gates were already opened. She now was excited for the secrets of Spring . . . and Summer . . . and Fall. She sensed in herself and where she lived something different. She wasn't living in a huge playground for her sole entertainment anymore. She looked around and noticed she now lived in a huge classroom where she made up the test and graded it herself. She couldn't stop smiling because she knew she was right.

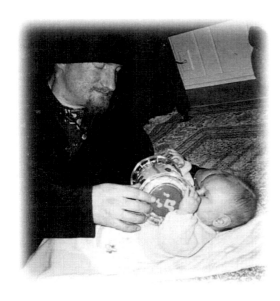

Today I watched a frog. I watched a tiny tiny frog jump out of an old log.

It had long tiny legs, big alert eyes, and a funny folded finger like Mommy stealing a nose. I smiled when it jumped closer. It looked around, blinked, looked up, blinked; then turned and jumped back to the comfort of the log.   I smiled again and said "Goodbye Ellie, have a nice day."   Today I watched a frog.

Maybe tomorrow you'll be a bunny.

Take care little Papoose.
— *Uncle TwoFeet*

We were in the wrong place at the wrong time. Turns out the wrong place was central Wisconsin, and the wrong time was just after dawn. Who would have thought that central Wisconsin could produce such a frightening place. Mikko and I proved Wisconsin could actually produce a near death place.

This was one moment among many that I was glad Mikko had wolf blood in his ancestry, and that I was born in the year of the dog.

We were on a volunteer assignment searching for a plane that was presumed to have crashed. My fourpawed companion and I were qualified and prepared for searching the most remote areas. We were assigned an area just North of an old abandoned quarry. From the access road it took Mikko and I about an hour to reach the quarry. The geography of the land was old hard wood with thick undergrowth. Tough going. When we eventually arrived to the openness of the quarry we were thankful for the fresh air. Be careful for what you're thankful for.

Fortuitously, I put Mikko back on his leash. Otherwise he might have ran over to see if the big dog staring at us wanted to play. On the West side of the opening was a small ridge which extended along the tree line. In a gap between trees was where the wolf stood and watched us. At first glance I thought he might be alone, but small movement in the brush to both sides of him proved he wasn't alone. The next forty-five seconds elapsed in suspended time.

Mikko sat down in a submissive manner and I simply couldn't move. I watched the wolf glare at us. It felt like being scanned by a MRI. Friend, Foe, or Food were the only possible results. This was one moment among many that I was glad Mikko had wolf blood in his ancestry, and that I was born in the year of the dog.

After about two thousand heartbeats, the big alpha seemed to have made his decision. With a very subtle head nod, two soldier wolves on both sides stood up. The alpha started to walk parallel along the ridge, not toward us. However, he never took his stare off us. Somehow I understood that we were being granted a pass, as long as we got the hell out of his hunting grounds. Mikko and I began to walk back toward the trail that brought us to this place.

I don't know how they did it, but when they did it felt like being the enemy in a chapter of Art of War. Probably while the alpha held us in his glare, he had more soldiers on the move. No matter, as soon as we started walking back to the trail two more wolves stood up on the opposite side of us. We were flanked the entire time. One small nod  from Chief Mouth Full of Teeth and we were essentially lunch. No escape plan was possible. We couldn't out run, couldn't out climb, couldn't out fight. All we could do was accept the pass and walk slowly back from whence we came. Vulnerability would have been a gross understatement at the time.

As it turned out, Mikko and I might have been in the wrong place at the wrong time; but we fortunately had the right credentials and the right amount of karma in the bank. Those forty-five seconds remained suspended for about the next thirty minutes, but we did make it back safe. Being prepared while searching unknown geography is sound common sense, but it will always be trumped by the unexpected.

You ever hear a tree talk? You ever been walking in the park or woods and think you hear your name? You ever think it might be true? It is. Trees, animals, and some types of produce can talk. Alright, maybe not the produce, but trees and animals can.

They speak the language of the wind. It's kind of like listening to an opera in a language you can't understand. However, you can follow the story through the tone and gestures. Windy—angry, barking--upset, cloudy—sad, et cetera. While in the park or the woods there is always an opera singing. The oak and the wolf might be the stars; but add in the birds, crickets, and frogs and Nature becomes a very noisy place.

When people speak, it tends to sound like an infomercial you can't put on mute. When the oak outside your window, or the dog lying on your bed speaks, it sounds like the Discovery channel. I knew a little German in high school, was almost fluent in Chinese at college, and I routinely speak English; but since we moved rural the birds and plants reminded me of my native tongue. If you listen patiently, Nature is everybody's native tongue. Say hello to the oak outside your window and tell it about your day.

It's kind of like listening to an opera in a language you can't understand.

...letters home

We're parents again! Sort of. But there's no way it's what
you think. It's not even what I think. We return from
Waterville in the a.m. where we needed more varnish. The
gang needs to walk until they're tired so they can kennel all
afternoon. [Middlenote: the Hansens did leave with their
dogs and one item left in barter is a functional 6x8 chainlink
kennel. Its set up opposite the main one, past the sidewalk,
on the tree line, with the gas tank as its neighbor.] We
return from the walk and are just about to pass the small
kennel when suddenly this fuzzy grey rock picked up its head
inside the kennel with the door still shut. Surprise!!! with a
big amount of What! Before finding out what it is I had to
run the guys off. Safely in their kennel I return to find a
baby owl. My owl with his new girlfriend apparently had a
successful Spring. Why and how is their only child (common)
sitting inside a dog kennel? He can't fly, barely waddles, and
the closest known nest is thirty-yards behind the kennel. I
approach and he sort of cowers and I notice no visible
injuries. ???????? I go inside the house and observe
through the window. The strange dance begins. The mother
appears in the tree above. Ever try to out wait an owl? Don't
bother. I find some chores to do; the dishes get done and I
check, still the same; make bedroll, still same; clean litter
boxes, still nothing. ?????? I decide to call for advice. Sheriff
transfers me through to DNR. The assistant tells me
without knowing owl type they can't and won't do anything
(and won't come to identify). After she bluntly suggests to
let Nature take its course, she suggests to move the baby out into

a clear area because she has known owls to swoop down and retrieve

fallen young. Owls are my favorite flying predator, and even as a helpless looking baby I find out fast why. I go up to it (softball size with fuzz) with a shovel thinking to scoop it up and walk it to the pond. The shovel touches his feet and his, talons are already literally my hand size. As I marvel, he starts to snap his beak together. No hooing, no meak squawk, a snapping chomp. Now the marveling stops real quick. His mother swoops in behind me, unbeknownst to me, lands on a branch fifteen feet above my head, and starts to swear at me in no known owl tone and not nice at all. Having my full attention I turn to explain and all I see is a pissed off mother owl with a six foot wing span right above me! I luckily am able to move without a heartbeat and comically put the shovel on my head like a helmet and run. From the "perceived" safety of the house I watch. The door of kennel was left open and I watched the mother observe her baby to be alive, then scan patiently for any other foe in the area. Good lord they're patient. She flies off and the baby stands and waddles through the door like Yoda. Trying to convince he's not so weak to abandon? Trying to follow mother? It takes three hours but he walks from the kennel, behind the garage, thirty feet parallel the driveway, and into the road ditch where I found him sitting on the last patch of grass before the heavily traveled dirt road. Helpless looking, he appeared as a sad member of our food chain waiting to play his part. I looked and noticed that from his point A to point B it was almost a straight line,

and through thick underbrush. He was apparently going
out with a lions fight. During his journey, I checked on him
every so often to see if I could stop him in a clearing still
thinking his mother would come pick him up. More
impressive stuff here: every time I walked out the door to
find him I would be flanked by his parents. And not from
distant branches. My owl friend who approved my presence,
would follow us on walks, was known to only land on the
uppermost canopy, tease the dogs into chasing him, and
occasionally reaffirm his majesty with fly-bys over the
skylights to cast his impressive wingspan, was now hunting
me. Cool. Wait, not cool. Every time I found baby one parent
would land on the nearest tree, and the other would circle
high above making sure I wasn't partnered either. Ten hours
and counting. Definitely not abandonment, plus I couldn't
figure out how such powerfully armed raptors were going to
swoop down and pick up their baby safely. The DNR was
wrong. The baby stayed on the fringe of the ditch and just
so a redneck in a pick-up wouldn't play a part of natural
selection I built a retaining wall of cinder blocks like a
concrete nest. Being well past dusk and believe you me, the
wall was built blindly because my attention was far above
the ground. I congratulated him on his bravery then went
to bed planning to either scoop the remains up off the road in
the morning, or scowl at those damn coyotes. 6:00 a.m. still
there. Time for second opinion on "let nature take its course"
A couple vets, an animal shelter, rescue haven, then the U of
M raptor center--bingo. Finally you can almost stop
scrolling. I don't have a Greathorned (didn't really believe so

but nice thought) I have a family of Bard owls. They mate longterm and he had to defend his territory from other males this whole time so they all understood when he went courting and brought back his mate, the menu was for his family. The pack and I were just helping him do it. The baby was a normal procedure. They grow too fast in the nest so they are relocated to the ground and the parents bring him his food. The little guy's journey to the ditch was just him following his mother's commands to where she wanted him. He didn't cross because of my wall; he didn't

cross because mother said not to. Plus I can attest to no predator trying to get close enough. I think this is really grand, but I need to remain partnered up with my owl. Having ganged up on me was just an unexpected necessity. From now on they alternate sleeping, hunting, and babysitting. I need to watch two hunting dogs, a natural Doby defender, and a cute little hole digger. The baby keeps getting moved around I guess, so all walks until I see three shapes in the canopy need to be short leashed or scouted thoroughly. It didn't help my first day on baby watch was 90 degrees. This entire lengthy memo needed to be constantly toweled off from the sweat drips. Small price for a family of Bard owls staying next door. I'm already loading the camera for the owl scrapbook, and grinning a bit 'cuz the coyotes just became a little less of a nuisance. That's all from the woods, got to go check for a snapping rock in the weeds, and give the gang their tick bath.

Bye, Pops, luv ya, 2'

A Thought

...The clincher is that I earned my cosmic PH-D's at Kilkenny, and I really feel I found EaglePine as a project and purpose for my first assignment. What I've been doing this past year is creating a place that accepts a cosmic voice, peace, and harmony and that promotes karma in the world. All should seek that for where you live. I am a caregiver bottomline, which involves my family, friends, animals and land. I know it sounds sappy, but the world where I live is full of sap. Let me know Smiles if that's enough to work with.

Hope you're having a positive day,
lator gator, Love you. 2'

Bean Soup

Had your bean soup tonight for dinner (Sunday). Very nice.
I really liked the large chunks of peeled tomatoes. To adjust
for taste, I added a scoop of my patented green-tea rice to
soak up the nice broth, and a hefty tablespoon of hot picante
to leave a tingly aftertaste. And now I'm inspired. I got the
crock pot out, washed it clean, and made a grocery list. I think
the tomatoes got me in a stew mood; so I plan to add some
baby potatoes, some corn, my carrot/celery combo, and maybe
a jalapeno or three to the twelve-bean starter kit. Any
personalized ingredients in your recipe I need to honor? I'm
also excited 'cuz Fred's just put watermelon on sale too. Add
a box of Ritz and our new menu is set for awhile. Just
wanted to say thanks for the cafeteria catalyst, and thanks
again for being the father you are.

Have a good day, eve, or morn;
talk at'cha with a tale or two soon.

Grackles

A tale from the woods--6:00 am and we're out for our walk.
One hour in the woods then back for dishes, sweeping, maybe
the litter boxes, and Mike Morris at 7 (KFAN show).

The creek is shallow so we follow that around the corner. A
nice sunrise, a good breeze, no smell of fertilizer . . . a good
morning. A flock of grackles appears. Must be over two
hundred and they fill all the surrounding canopy. They squawk
in this harmonized orchestra of cacophony. Usually a
displeasing sound but that morning was different. I listened
like they were talking to us. I've always felt like the trees were
gossiping all around us but that morning the birds simply
made sense. I knew at that moment that English was my
second language. I speak it, write it, read it, understand most
of it; but I have to work at it; like translating Chinese. When I
look at an animal, or listen to the breeze blow through the trees,
or study a flock of black birds the sound of Nature just comes
natural. The problem with people is they speak too much and

not listen enough. The language of Life requires listening. I wish people would listen to the trees around them more, to practice speaking Nature. I think we would all understand each other more often if we listen to the dog, cat, owl, krackel, frog, horse, goat, etcetera. I

speak English but I am a fluent member of the backyard. More is said with a tweak of the eye than any thousand-word dissertation. The crying Indian, the laughing grandma, the determined horse coming down the home stretch (how 'bout that War Emblem ?!)--all deserve doctorates in expression. That's all from the woods.

Say hi to your eagle on the island
and the ducks in your trees. 2'

postscript--

hi pops, just thought I'd pass along a journal entry. You expressed you wanted to hear some of what I think about. This is a sample of the soundbits I hear each day. I have a bunch more if you're interested. You know you worry too much, and you said you worry 'bout my isolation down here. No worries. If I could construct a perfect day it would involve watching the sunrise, taking care of animals, not interacting with anybody, and sitting on a log for three hours waiting for the moon to rise above the trees. You've not raised a normal son. What you have is somebody that is so at peace with myself and the world around me that I don't question much--I just enjoy observing. I live each day knowing that it's going to involve setbacks, mistakes, disappointments, and the occasional injury, but I also know every day will offer those few moments of profound beauty. A butterfly landing on a branch right before my face defines my day, not the feeding and cleaning and broken knuckles. I gladly pick up all the poop because birds will sing to me sometime today. In short,

I'm a problem solver who enjoys his five minutes of silence. Now, let's get on to the real worries of Tim's studio, Molly's yard, and where your garden is going to go. I hope this makes sense, I don't write down my ideas much, I usually just discuss them in my head.

Have a good day and give Mickey a treat if she shows up today. 2' and the FourPaws Gang.

Shopping in the Woods

Hi Pops! How goes the vernal equinox for 'ya? It's all mud and yellow snow down here. Writing to relay an unexpected gift I was given the other day. Its pre-dusk and I'm walking the brood around for their pre-dinner walk-a-bout. Mikko stops without warning--no sound or movement that I could decipher--and stares up into the tree canopy. Sure enough, Mikko was paying silent homage to his antagonist the Owl; whom, by the way, has matured over the winter and tolerates others more, or is a different Owl who won this prime territory 'cause he (?) kept sitting on his branch even as the other dogs and I caught up to Mikko. Anyway, this majestic scene was enough of a significant moment that I figured that was our Earthly lullaby and we should accept it and continue. The background information of this scene is that I was artistically stymied that very morning while working on some new walking sticks. My style is either improving or simply changing, but I couldn't figure out why

I was so not approving of what to do with the new wood.
So, after the Owl we circled around and headed back to the
kennel for dinner. Fritz got wind of something down by the
road and made a bee-line to the ditch. Before Roxanne could
catch up to her tag partner Fritz was already coming back.
However, he came back with something in his mouth. Like
a true lab mix, he brought it right to me. I had him drop it
and noticed it was a bird carcass. A few wacks to remove the
snow and it turned out to be a decapitated hawk. A hawk
carcass with all of its feathers intact. It was a clean kill
without any post-meal damage. I brought it inside, took it
downstairs, and it turns out the brown pattern of the
feathers matches wonderfully with the wood grain of the
new sticks. I now have a pile of enchanted feathers to ordain
a new series of walking sticks. Like PaiPai paying rent with
the occasional mouse/bird/rabbit installments, I think our
new Owl just bought himself the prime roost of our little
oasis. I love shopping in the woods. Well, that's my yarn for
today. Hope all is kosher up yonder.

Type to 'ya later, TwoFeet.

Johnson Compound

Hi- How goes the evening? It's wet and sullen down here. I'm typing to clarify a few quick points in case Ma misconstrued some references. Yes, indeed I had an epiphany. Our little oasis seems to be going the way of mountain gorillas, panda bears, and our National Parks...suffocation via humanity. The week long installation of the electric lines felt like sitting around the campfire and listening to the bulldozers plow their way through the underbrush. We love it here, and it's been a grand education with tremendous professors. The Chief seems to think though, that we've learned and observed as much as we can. I just need to stick around and do a bit of post-grad work. No matter what becomes of this spiritual vortex however, its lessons need to be preserved. I need to paint the walls of the cave. When we do eventually move (not anytime on the horizon) it'll be to another sanctuary with a larger life expectancy. I envision something like you wrote about. Enough land so hikes don't become redundant; a water source where swimming and fishing are common experiences; a household that visitors would describe as rustic; an area for a barn so the goats can get out of the weather; perhaps a plot for an orchard; a meadow where Ellie and her cousins can catch grasshoppers; and a night sky that is void of artificial light and sound. Not entirely attainable, but something that resembles it. If it needs to start with just the land, hard work is no deterrent. Until then I intend on doing everything I can that utilizes my ability to translate Nature into human speak. I'm open for suggestions and advice. I never said I was an island, I think I did say something like a peninsula though. You mentioned helping the family business. I'd love to help where I could, but I don't want horselady jobs that are created just so I won't turn somewhere else. I know I can excel at any normal job or career, but my life passion pulses just to the left of normal. The only thing I struggle at is how to market that skill. I welcome any support or advice. For work, I'll do anything part-time, but for career work I need to  use my ability to translate Nature: writing, lecturing, teaching. In the end (or in the future I guess), I am a caretaker at heart. I want to do what I'm able so I can exist in peaceful solitude, send you guys on random cruises, ensure nieces and nephews book learnin' and tree learnin', and maybe prevent just a wrapper or two from being littered out the car window. Well, that's my re-clarification in case Ma cliffnoted any statements. We'll talk more about it later. Sunday's storm caused much downfall damage (just to the trees, nothing else), so today I go forth with axe and saw again and try to clear the trails. It wouldn't be so necessary if I didn't have leash dogs. Its either spend three hours parting the barked seas or three hours unwrapping dogs from around them. Oh well, hope all is well slightly up North.   Takecare and talk to 'ya later. 2'

Resume Synopsis

Why consider me for your position? Because I am qualified for the task. My qualifications are as follows: I am ambitious enough to have owned and/or directed six different companies [Sunset Landscaping, InFunStructure, Teen Quest, Streefland Ropes Course, Just 'cause, and FourPaws et Cetera]. I have the will enough to have made a solo bike trek from Minneapolis, Mn. to Austin, Tx. I have the skill enough to have risen to the highest level wherever I've been employed. I am humble enough to start at the lower levels; including caring for developmentally challenged autistic adults where the room needed to have tables bolted to the floor, and the chairs chained to the tables, and where you never wear clothes to work you would like to wear back home. Also, I am creative enough to sell handmade walking sticks at the Minnesota Arboretum. I am caring enough to set aside my own needs for those of my four dogs and three cats. I am physically and ethically strong enough to volunteer personally to turn 80 acres of wooded property into 3.5 miles of hiking trails for the Soluna Retreat Center. Again, I am qualified for your position.

Please consider me. Thank you.

Unwanted Holiday Memory

So, last night was the second night that the white one and the small one were on timeout and had to sleep in the kennel. Obviously leaving the doby and the lab. More room in bed right? That's what I figured; finally some blanket-time. Never assume I guess. Well you remember I have this habit of being a spinning sleeper. I start on my back, quarter-turn to on my side looking Right, quarter-turn to on my stomach looking Right, simple flip of the head so still on stomach looking Left, turn to be on side again, back to the back, et cetera. Well, bedtime arrives, Daddy slides in first, Shania waits until I lift the covers to slide in underneath to about my knees. Gibson usually goes to the foot of the bed and curls in the corner, leaving Kismet on the wall near my head (Roxanne has insomnia so she roams all about). A well oiled system. Until two of them aren't there. Anyway good sleepysleep for most of the night and about 4:30 I end up on my side

looking Right. A few moments later I'm awakened by this paw being draped over my shoulder. I look back and see that Gibson has rolled over a couple of times and is right behind me . . . on his side. What's the matter here? I was spooning with my dog! Like any guy would, I woke him up and made him wrestle around for awhile to right a wrong. I don't care about their offense anymore; the other two still have small rations and no hike time, but will be allowed back in bed tonight.

Hope all is a cool breeze on a sunny day for you,
love you, later. 2'

Spring Fling (excerpt)

*If I read a good book, I cannot tell you the main characters'
names, or where it took place; but I can describe the colors in
the room when he refuses to leave her side, and the sounds
that resonate during the first rainfall which will save the
crops. All I know is that Spring showed up for us last week.
Our new season of rebirth, green leaves, and small things
that fly is bringing with it Unity this season. It started with
the Full Moon. It showed up not as a dominating lunar
sphere beaming through cloudy skies, but as a proud
chaperone for an endless choir of stars. With an immediate
response were the coyotes. They didn't take turns yelping
homage; instead they sang acapella in unison. Next, Dawn
escorted the new turkey brood. Gobbles in the grass, gobbles
in back of the barn, and still more from the roadside over
the hill. Not smart for tasty birds to let everything know
where they are hiding, but certain occasions prove the*

exception rule. Then the geese fly by like kaleidoscope aerial Paul Reveres announcing the approaching season. And just that morning the grackles prowled the canopy letting all

observers know that they're not as pretty as butterflies, but still a lot better than locust. Hard to argue with sure signs. I don't remember the signs from last year, and I'm sure to forget who showed up when this year; but the messenger  is never really the important part. So, for whatever it's worth... Spring is here and it's not alone.

Enjoy, share, and takecare.
TwoFeet and his FourPaws.

DEATH OF EAGLEPINE

> He showed us Nature's beauty and the will to survive.

Died of strong winds and weak roots, our inspiration and namesake, EaglePine. He lived a long and noble life. He showed us Nature's beauty and the will to survive. He figured he could be more of an influence living in our memories and show greater strength through our words. He is survived by his small adoptive family; a forked Birch sapling, several tiny offspring, a protective bramble bush, and a flourishing berry bush. Perhaps all EaglePine Review readers should plant at least one tree to honor our founding inspiration. Live strong, learn to survive, and always notice Nature's beauty.

Later Gator, - 2'
6.16.70 to 9.19.07